Learn to Carve a

COWBOY

Pattern drawing by John Allard.

ISBN 978-1-56523-576-2 (kit)

ISBN 978-1-56523-619-6 (booklet only)

To learn more about the other great books from Fox Chapel Publishing, or to find a retailer near you, call toll-free 800-457-9112 or visit us at ***www.FoxChapelPublishing.com.***

Note to Authors: We are always looking for talented authors to write new books in our area of woodworking, design, and related crafts. Please send a brief letter describing your idea to Acquisition Editor, 903 Square Street, Mount Joy, PA 17552.

Second Printing
Printed in China

Learn to Carve a

Cowboy

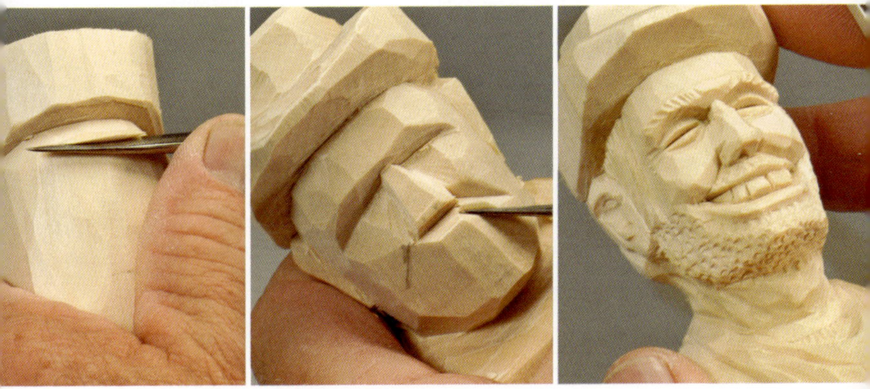

HAROLD ENLOW

FOX CHAPEL
PUBLISHING

Learn to Carve a Cowboy

Cowboy caricatures have a long history in America, dating back to the classic work of Andy Anderson, who is credited as one of the earliest American caricature carvers. Even today, broken-down cowboys find their way into almost every carving competition and most popular instructors offer rough-outs of cowboys.

As with most caricatures, the success of the carving depends on a blend of realistic and exaggerated features. Most good caricature artists realize that you need to know how to create a realistic face in order to do a good caricature. It doesn't take much to turn a realistic carving into a caricature. On this cowboy, the ears are a little oversized and the teeth are slightly larger than normal. Both of these features give the carving a fun and happy look.

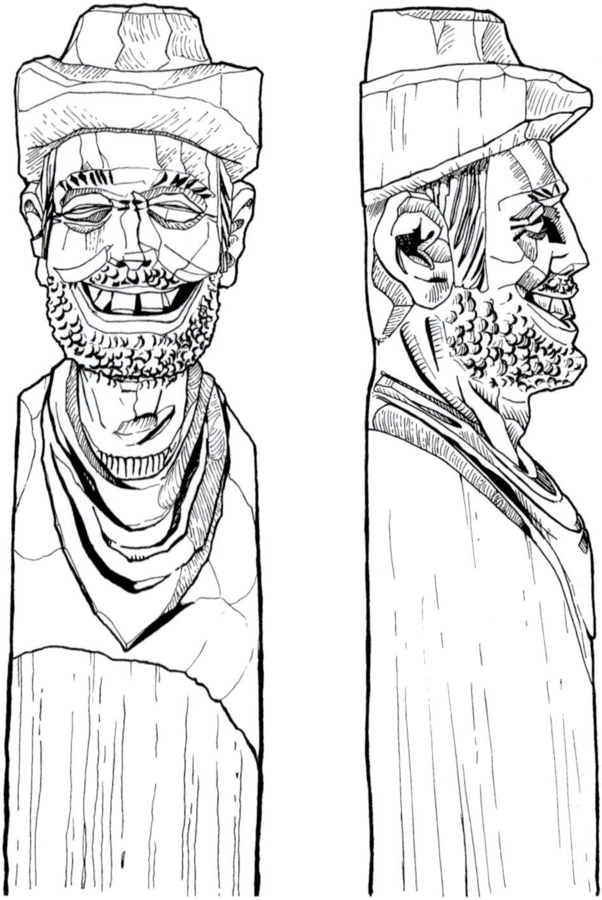

I have listed what tools I use for this carving, but you can use whatever tools you have on hand—there is no need to use the exact tools I mention as long as you are pleased with the end result.

Rough in the hat. Round the top of the blank. Stop-cut along the bottom of the hat line with a carving knife and carve up to the hat line to begin shaping the forehead.

Separate the chin from the neck. Stop-cut along the chin line with a carving knife and carve up to the stop cut to separate the chin from the neck. Begin to round the face. Leave wood in the middle of the face for the nose.

Rough out the top of the hat. Stop-cut along the top of the hat brim with a carving knife and carve up to the stop cut. Continue removing wood until you establish the large brim and small crown of the hat.

Rough in the sides of the face. Carve a notch around the hat brim on top of the ears. Then carve away the wood in the temples and in front of the ears with a ⅜" #3 gouge.

Remove the wood under the ears. Use a carving knife.

Shape the sides of the head. Taper the sides of the face toward the chin using a carving knife. Then thin the temple area to make the nose stick out more.

Rough in the ears. Use a #3 gouge to carve up alongside the ears to separate the ears from the face. Carve around the ears to isolate the ears from the rest of the head. The backs of the ears stick out more than the front of the ears, which blend into the sides of the face.

Outline the major facial features. Stop-cut along the brow line and at the bottom of the nose with a carving knife. Carve up to these stop cuts. The cut up to the brow line shapes the top of the nose. The cut up to the bottom of the nose begins to shape the bottom lip. Extend the cut along the brow line and rough in the eye sockets.

Rough in the nose. Stop-cut alongside the nose with a carving knife and cut up to the stop cut to separate the nose from the cheeks.

Add the smile lines. Stop-cut along the smile lines with a carving knife. Cut up to the stop cuts to free a wedge of wood to represent the smile lines.

11

Rough in the mouth and chin. Stop-cut along the cleft of the chin with a carving knife and carve down to the stop cut to create the mouth mound.

12

Add the sideburns. Sketch in the sideburns. Stop-cut along the sideburn with a 3/8" #3 gouge and then cut up to the stop cut to separate the sideburn from the face.

Separate the eyelids from the eye sockets. Carve along the inside corner of the eyelids using a V-tool to separate the eyelids from the eye sockets. Deepen the inside corner of the eye socket near the nose.

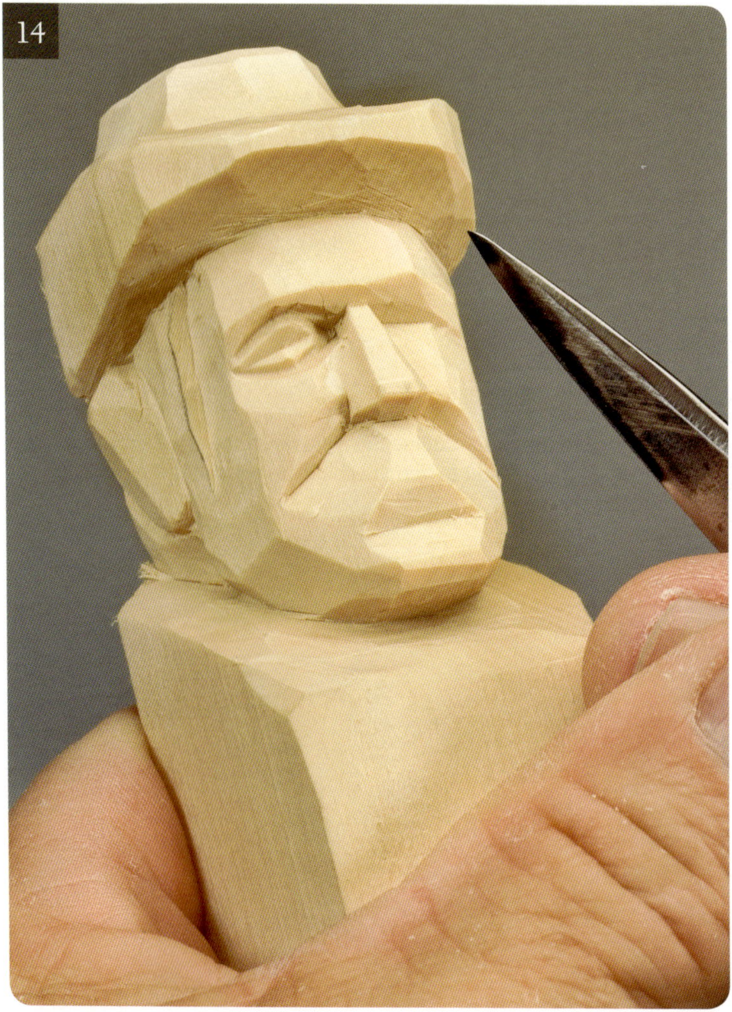

Clean up the eyes. Use the tip of a carving knife to clean up the eyelids and eye socket.

Add the wings to the nose. Outline the wings with the tip of a carving knife and carve up to the stop cut to free the chip. This separates the wings of the nose from the cheeks.

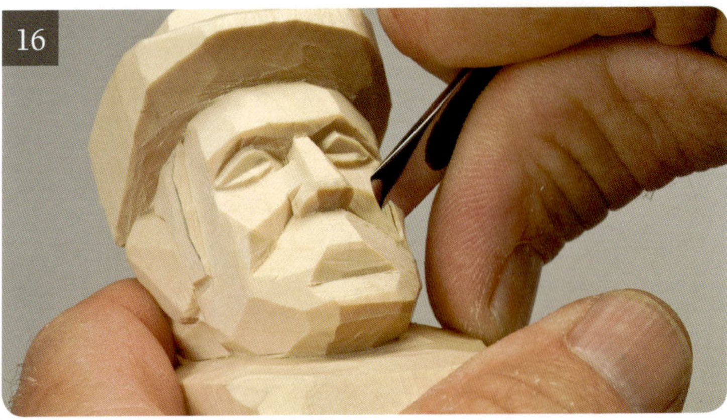

Round over the cheeks. Use a ⅜" #3 gouge upside down or a carving knife to round over the cheeks.

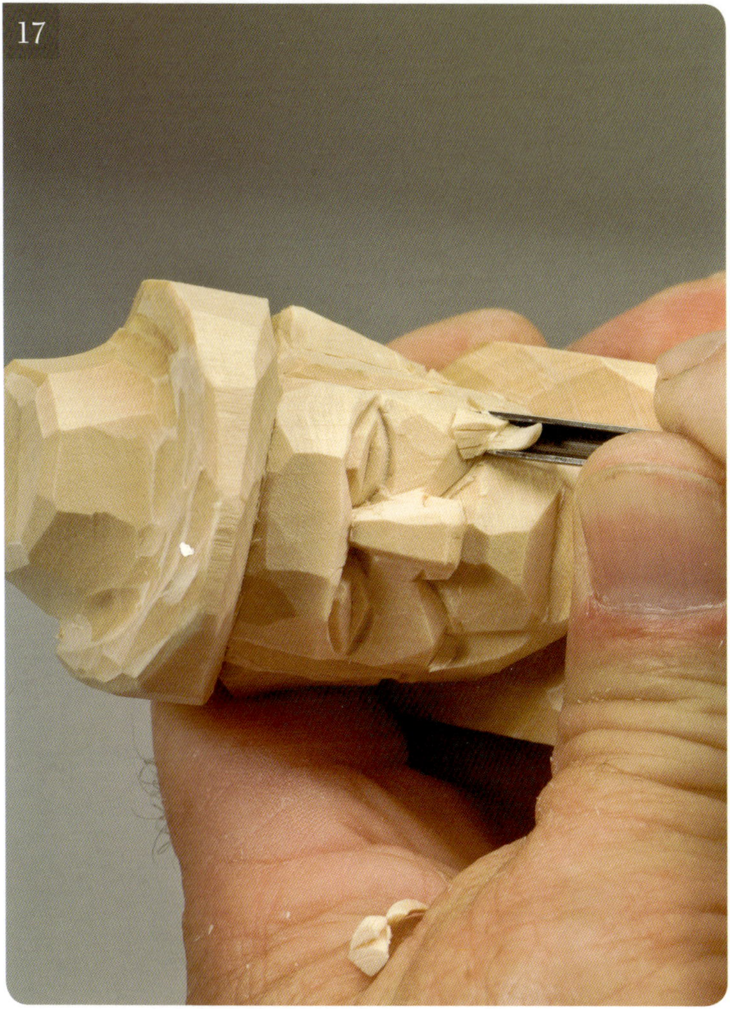

Finish shaping the cheeks. Deepen the smile lines using a 3mm veiner.

Carve the hole in the ears. Push and rotate a 3mm veiner in a circle to carve a small hole in the ears.

Carve under the ear. Use a knife to remove wood from under the ear to make the lobe of the ear stick out.

20

Carve the inside of the ear. Stop-cut along the internal structure of the ear. Taper your cuts inward so the cuts meet in the middle and free the chip.

Round the eyelids. Since the cowboy is squinting, and there is very little iris and pupil visible, the eyelids will cover most of the eye. Use a carving knife to round the eye down into the bottom of the V-tool cuts.

Rough in the mouth. Shape the mouth mound under the nose with a ⅜" #3 gouge. Draw in the line between the lips and carve along the line with a ⅛" V-tool.

Rough out the neck and chin. Use a carving knife, a veiner, and a ⅜" #9 gouge to remove the excess wood around the bandanna and the neck. Separate the chin from the neck and the neck from the bandanna.

Add the bandanna wrinkles. Draw in a series of J-shaped and reverse J-shaped lines. Carve along the lines with a ⅛" V-tool. Use a carving knife to recess the base of the neck area. Clean up the wrinkles with a 3⁄16" skew chisel. Carve the grooves representing the visible T-shirt collar with a ⅛" V-tool.

Carve the eyebrows. Carve a series of short lines with a ⅛" V-tool. Use the V-tool to add a few crow's feet.

Carve the squinting eyes. Carve between the eyelids with a small V-tool to create the squinting eyes. Deepen the cuts with a carving knife.

27

Carve the mouth. Stop-cut along the top lip and the bottom lip with a carving knife. Carve up to the stop cuts to separate the teeth from the lips. The deepest part is the corners of the mouth. Carve under the lower lip with a 3mm veiner to shape the lower lip.

28

Carve the teeth. Use the tip of a carving knife to carve small grooves to represent the teeth and the gaps between the teeth.

Finish carving the ear. Use a V-tool to carve the remaining grooves inside the ear.

Carve the sideburns. Use a V-tool to carve hair texture into the sideburns. Make sure the lines are curved.

Carve the whiskers. Carve across the grain with a micro gouge. Make short strokes. Push the gouge in and pop out the wood. Make sure you do not carve them into regular rows. Carve the tiny grooves randomly. Carve all over and under the chin. Then carve whiskers over the upper lip.

7 Fun and Festive Santas You Can Carve
WOODCARVING
ILLUSTRATED
HOLIDAY 2010 ■ ISSUE 53
Whittling
Ornaments
Quick-Carve
Stackable Snowman
Painting a
Duck Decoy
Super Simple
Sharpening
Best Design Contest
Results Announced
Showcasing 15 Winners and
13 Honorable Mentions
Cowboy
Bottlestopper

Carving Faces Workbook

Learn to Carve Facial Expressions with the Legendary Harold Enlow

By Harold Enlow

Follow along with Harold as he teaches you how to carve faces with life and expression.

ISBN: 978-1-56523-585-4

$19.95 • 144 pages

To order direct, call **800-457-9112** or visit *www.FoxChapelPublishing.com*

By mail, please send check or money order + $4.00 per book for S&H to:
Fox Chapel Publishing, 1970 Broad Street, East Petersburg, PA 17520